WHAT MAKES A MAGNET?

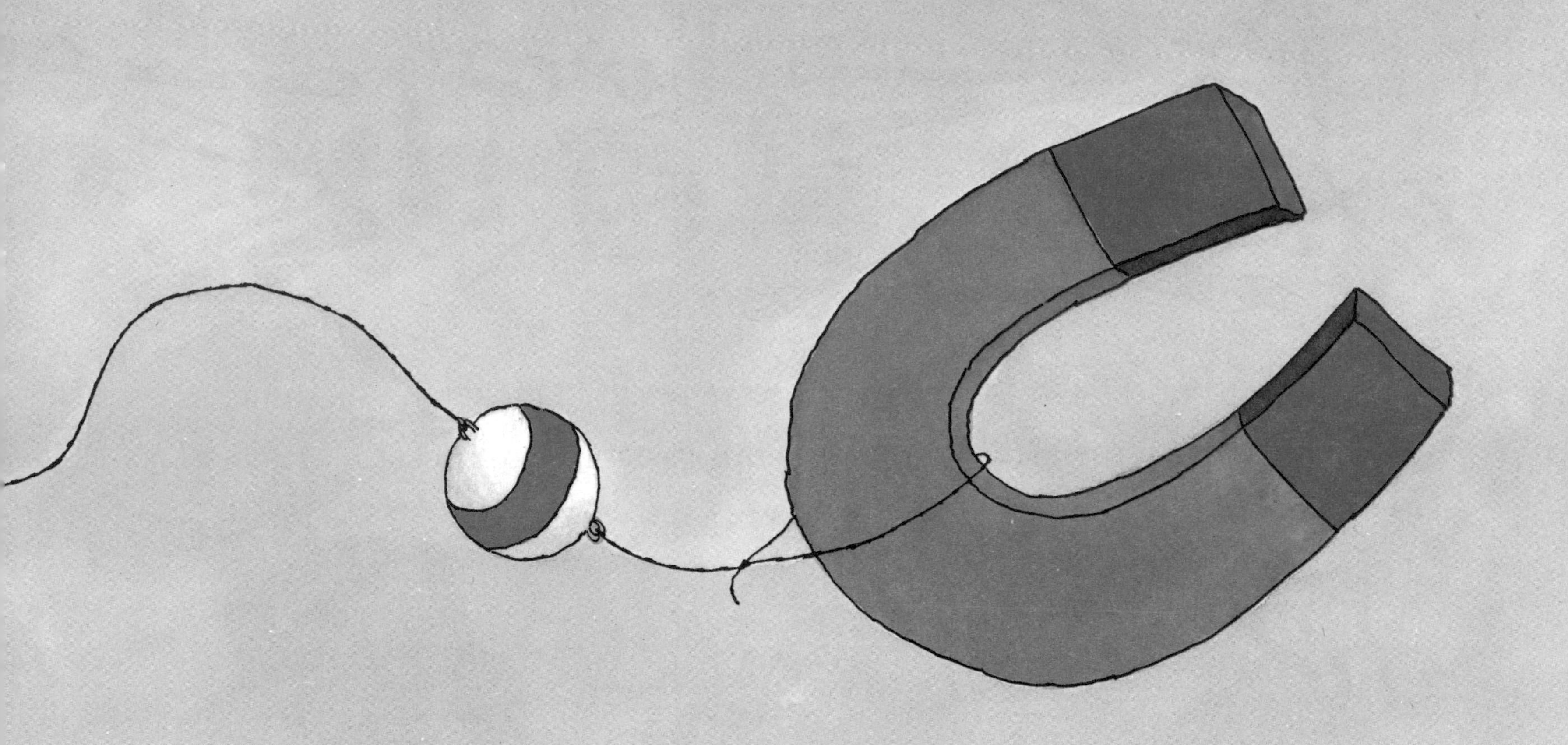

Let's go fishing with a magnet.

Put different things in a box: a penny, a nickel, and a dime; a twig, some tacks and paper clips, bits of aluminum foil, rubber bands, pieces of paper, and a pin or two.

Next, find a magnet. They come in different shapes and sizes.

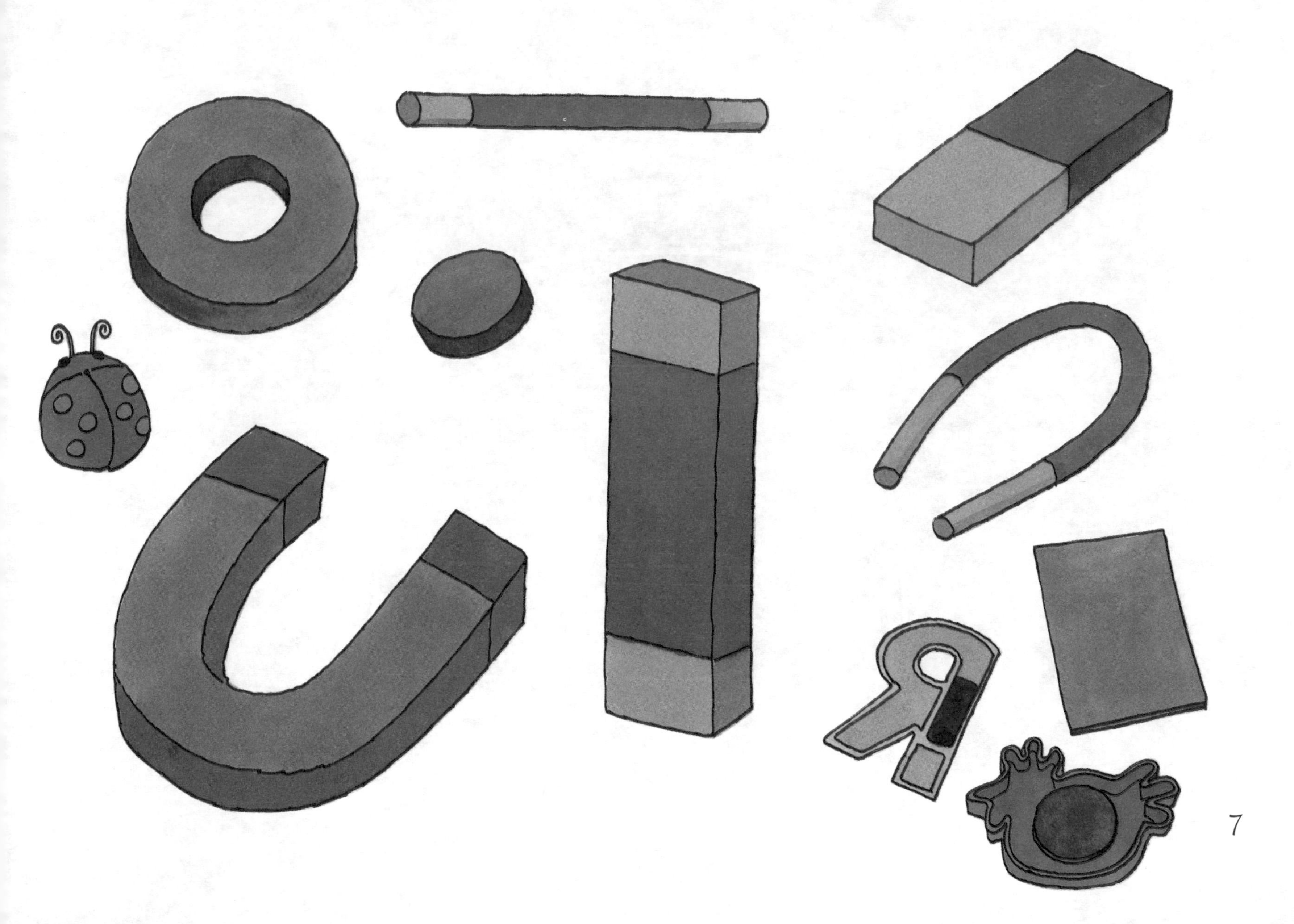

Tie one end of a string around your magnet. Tie the other end to a stick or a pencil. This is your fishing pole.

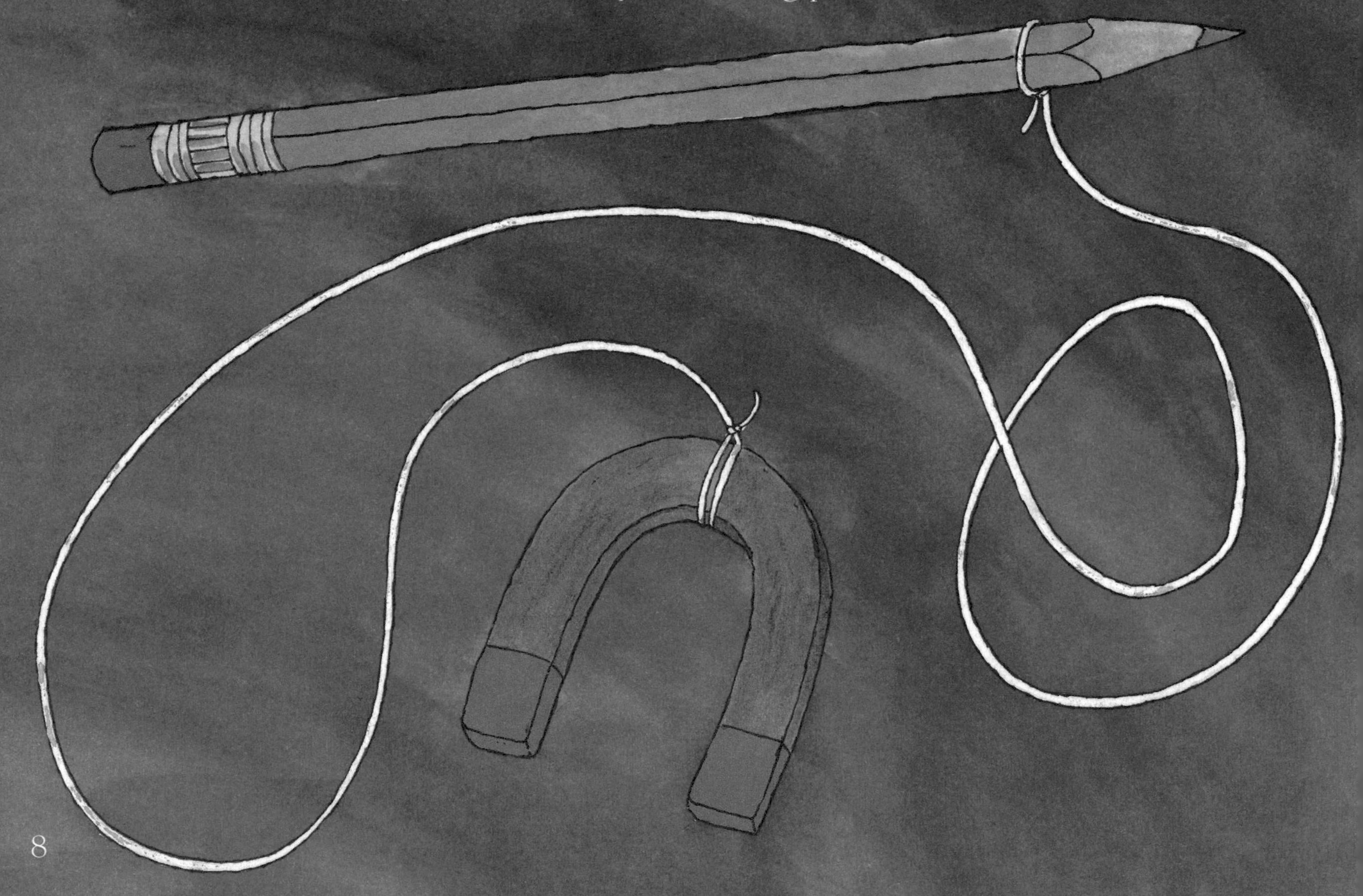

Go fishing in the box. Put the things you "catch" in a pile. The others will stay in the box.

Everything you lifted out of the box is made of iron: the tacks, the paper clips, and the pin. The magnet won't pick up a twig, rubber bands, aluminum foil, paper, a dime, a nickel, or a penny because they are not made of iron. Dimes, nickels, pennies, and aluminum foil are made of other kinds of metal. A magnet picks up only things that have a lot of iron in them.

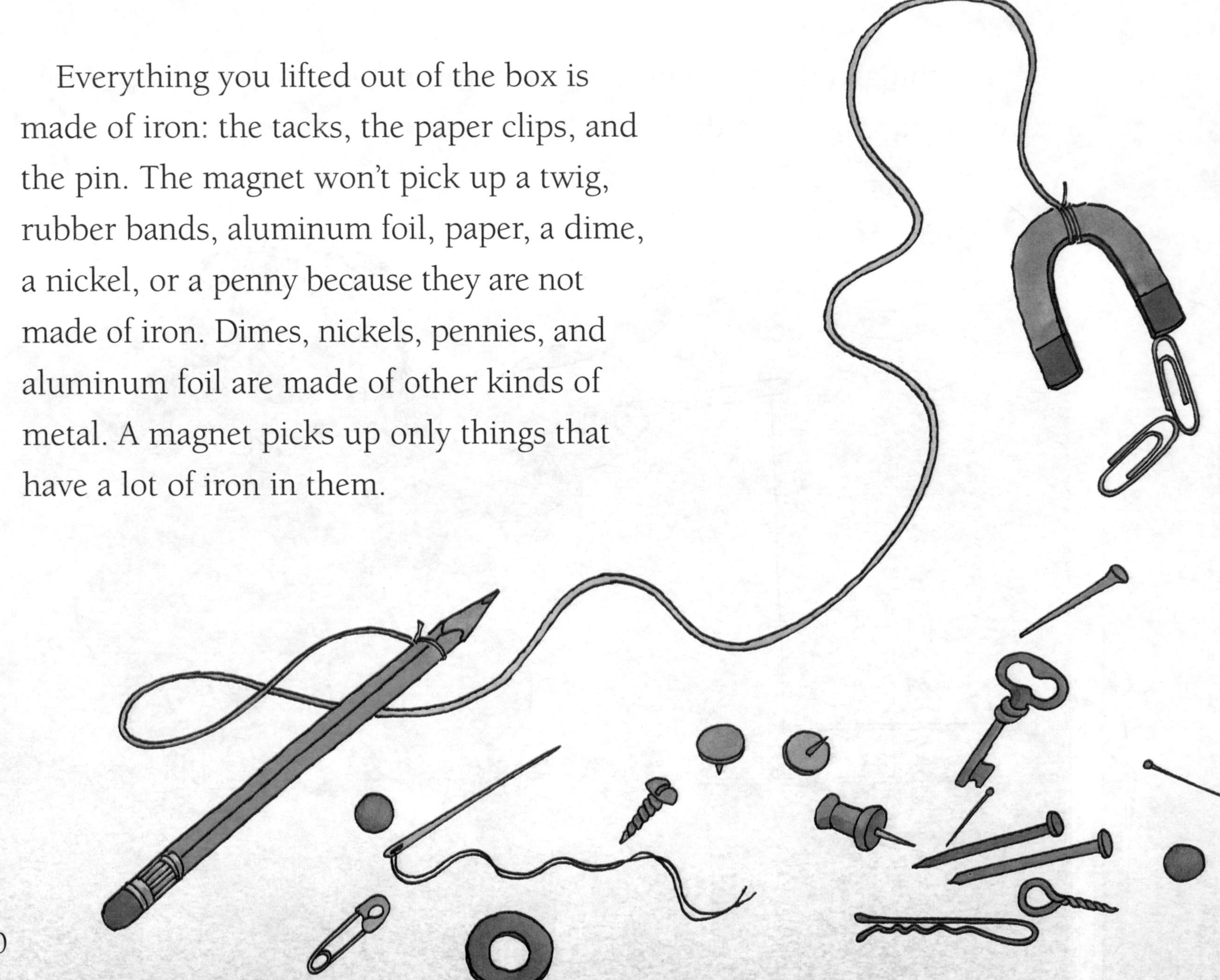

UBBLE
UM
ONE CENT

You can make your own magnet with a needle. Needles are made of steel, which is mostly iron.

Hold the eye of the needle.

Stroke the needle along one end of the magnet.

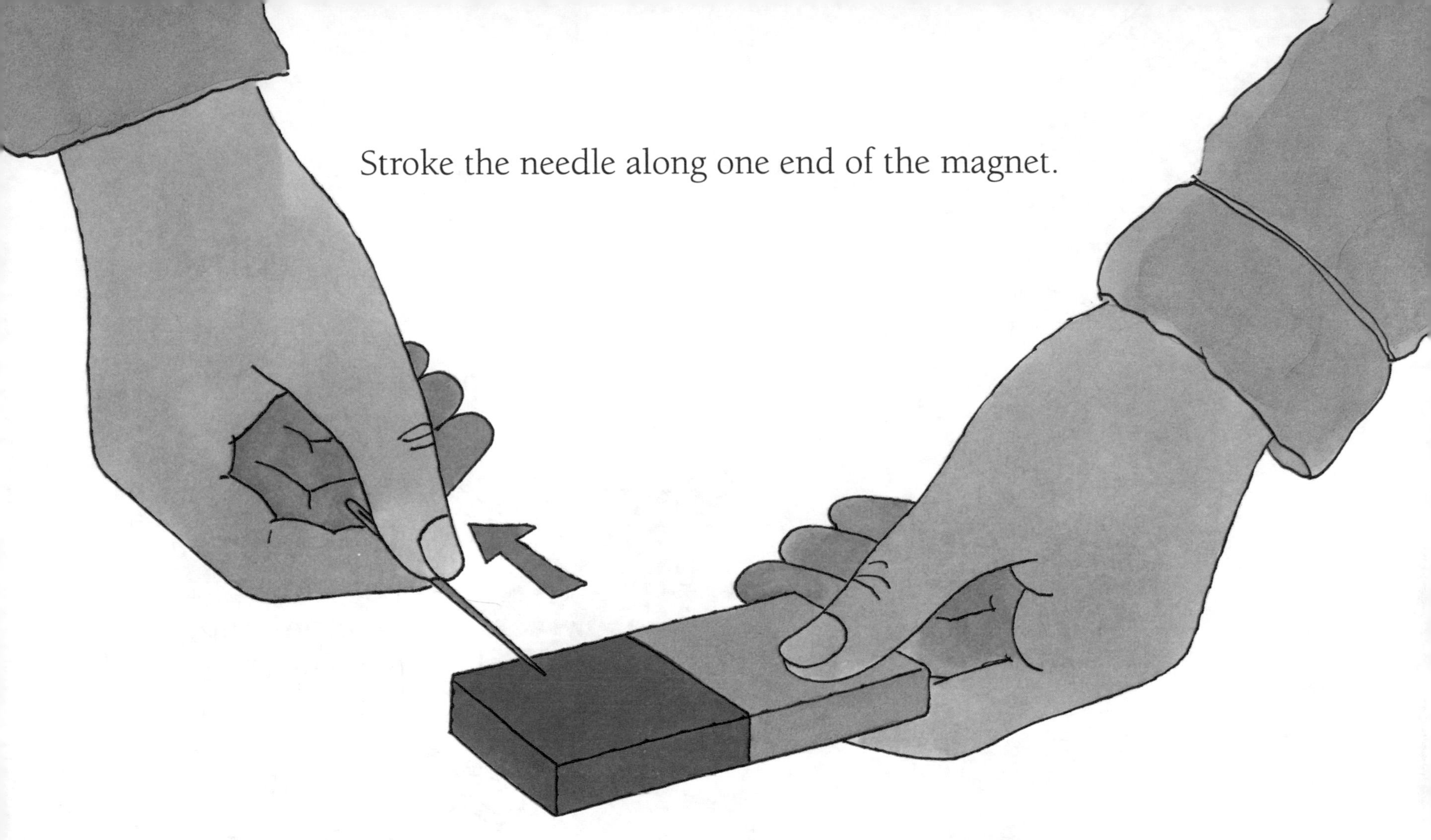

Move along the magnet in only one direction: from the eye of the needle to the point, not back and forth. Do this twenty or thirty times.

Touch the end of the needle to a tack, a paper clip, or another needle. Your needle will lift them up. You have made a magnet.

The bigger and stronger a magnet is, the more objects it will pick up at once.

A refrigerator door has a magnet around it that holds the door shut tight. The magnet is under the plastic strip around the door. Test it with a paper clip. The door will hold the clip.

ICE CREAM!
HI
PILLSBURY FREE LIBRARY
HOURS
TUES.....9-12
.....1-8
WED......2-5
THURS.....9-12
.....1-8
SAT.....9-12
Apples
potatoes
juice
nuts
eggs
sauce
beans
B
C
D
STRAWBERRIES
FROZEN LIMAS
FROZEN PEAS
MARK'S ICE CREAM
CHOCOLATE CHIP
MARK'S
ICE CREAM

Your needle magnet is a little one. But there are very large magnets. In fact, the whole Earth is a magnet. And you can prove it.

1

First, use your needle magnet to make a compass. Get two small pieces of foam plastic, or cork, and stick a piece on each end of the needle.

2

Then float the needle in a bowl of water. The needle will swing around so one end points north. Keep the needle in the center of the bowl, so it can swing freely. Turn the needle around. When you let go, the same end will again point north.

3

Put a dot of ink on that end. You have made a compass.

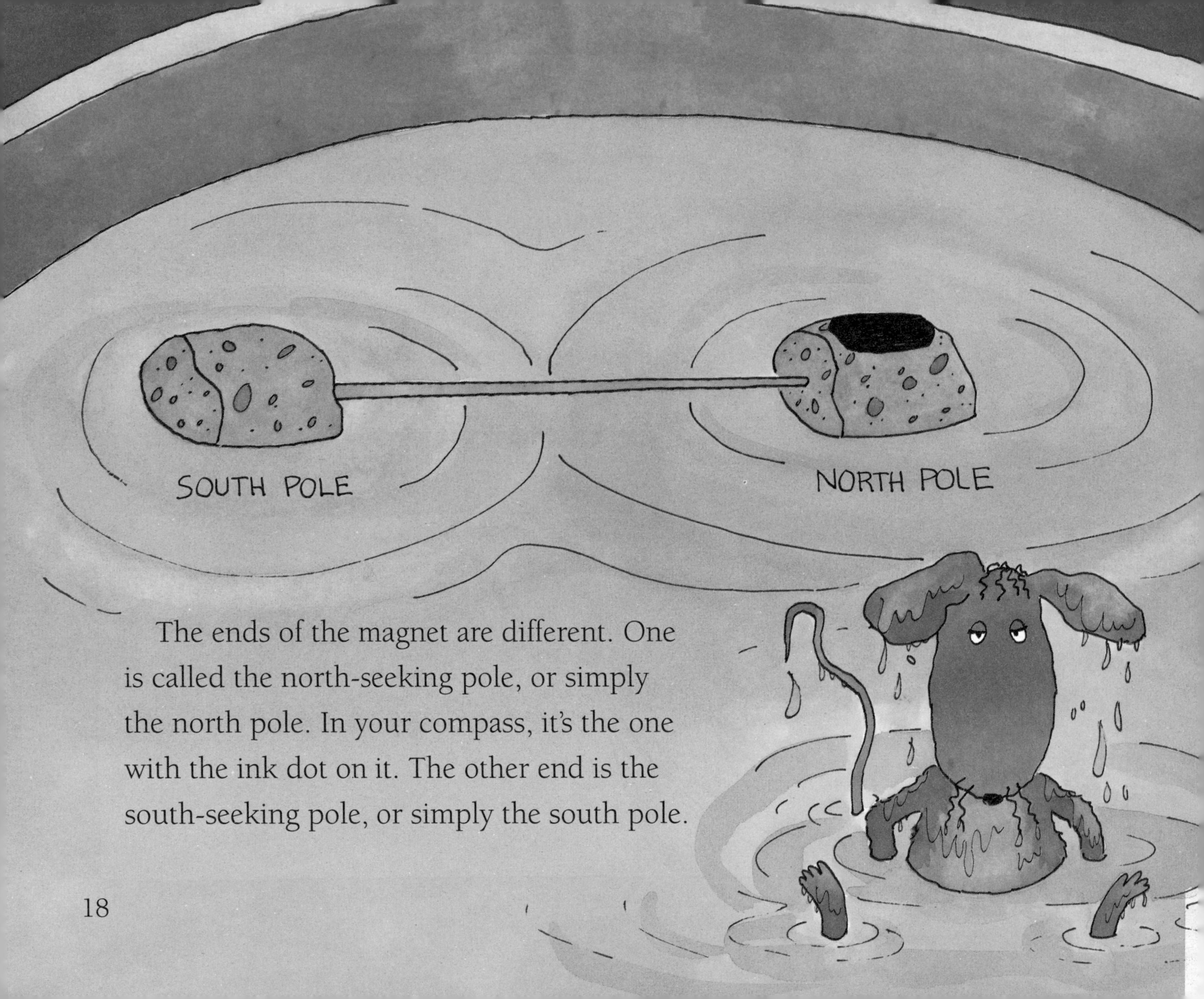

The ends of the magnet are different. One is called the north-seeking pole, or simply the north pole. In your compass, it's the one with the ink dot on it. The other end is the south-seeking pole, or simply the south pole.

Magnets are strongest at the poles. When you picked things out of your fishing box, they stuck to the ends of the magnet, not the middle.

Your compass points north because the Earth is a magnet. The north-seeking pole of your compass points toward the north pole of the Earth magnet. No matter how you turn your compass, it will always point north when you let go of it.

The Earth is a magnet because it contains a lot of iron. The moon does not have as much iron, so it is not a magnet. Your compass would not work on the moon.

When people go hiking in the woods, they take a compass with them so they don't get lost. It tells them which direction is north, so they can find their way back home.

Airplane pilots and ship captains also use compasses so they don't get lost.

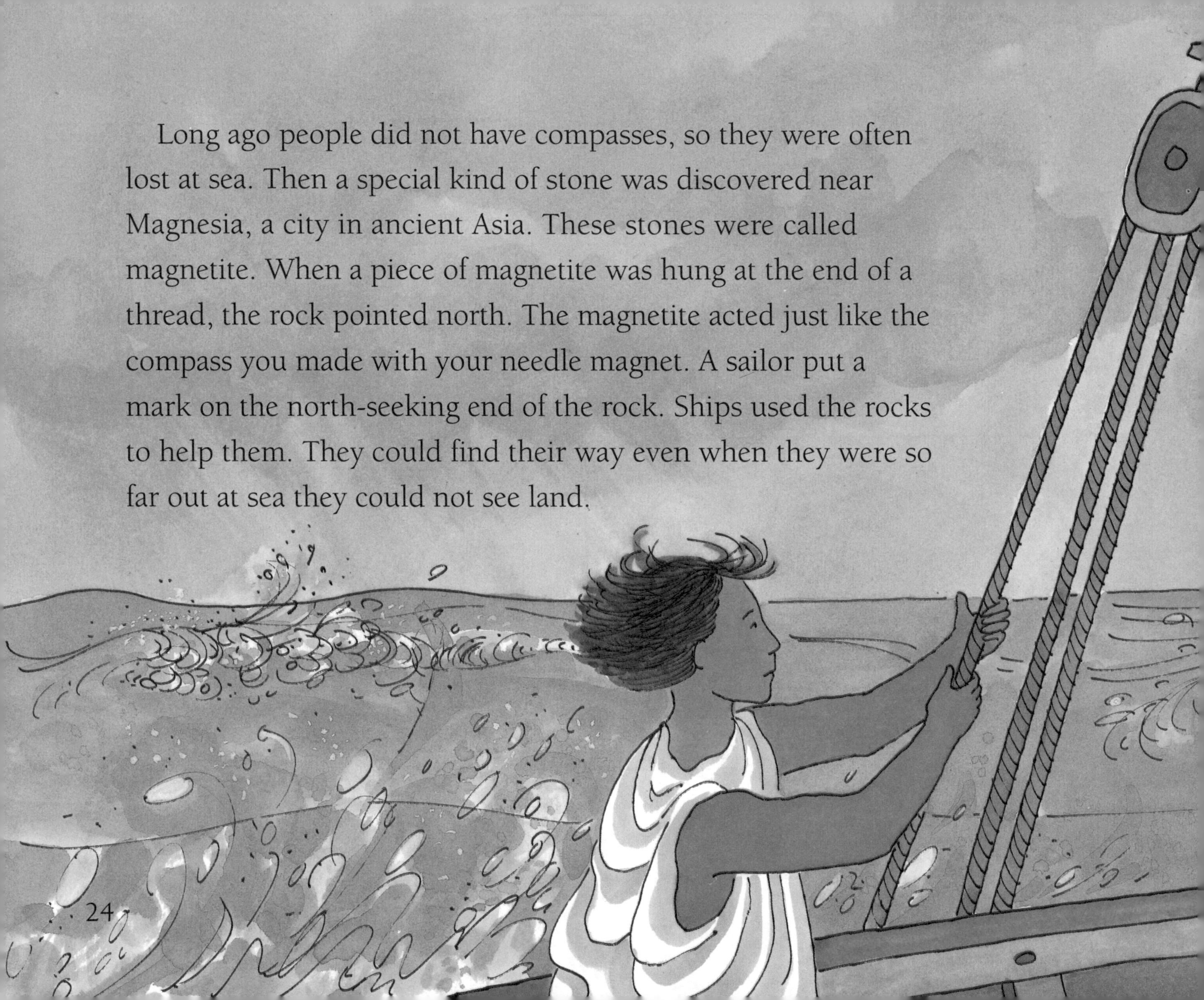

Long ago people did not have compasses, so they were often lost at sea. Then a special kind of stone was discovered near Magnesia, a city in ancient Asia. These stones were called magnetite. When a piece of magnetite was hung at the end of a thread, the rock pointed north. The magnetite acted just like the compass you made with your needle magnet. A sailor put a mark on the north-seeking end of the rock. Ships used the rocks to help them. They could find their way even when they were so far out at sea they could not see land.

Pieces of magnetite are natural magnets because they contain lots of iron, just as your needle does. Magnetite compasses were often called lodestones, or "leading stones," and you can see why.

Now that you have made a magnet and a compass, you can make even more discoveries.

Make another needle magnet, just as you made the first one. Move the point of your new magnet close to one end of the compass, the end with the ink-dot on it. Don't touch the compass. The compass may move toward the needle; it may be attracted. Or the compass might swing away from the magnet; it may be repelled.

You'll find that two north-seeking poles repel each other. Also, a north-seeking pole and a south-seeking pole attract each other. Like poles repel each other; unlike poles attract.

When you made your magnets, you used needles because they contain iron. Suppose you had tried to make a magnet using a penny or an aluminum nail? You could have stroked it across the magnet all day long, and it would never have become a magnet.

Why is that? Why can only iron become a magnet? Scientists are not sure why this is true. Maybe it's because the smallest bits of iron in a needle are like small magnets that point in all directions. When you stroke a needle across a magnet, the tiny magnets line up—the magnetism of one particle is added to another, making the magnetism stronger.

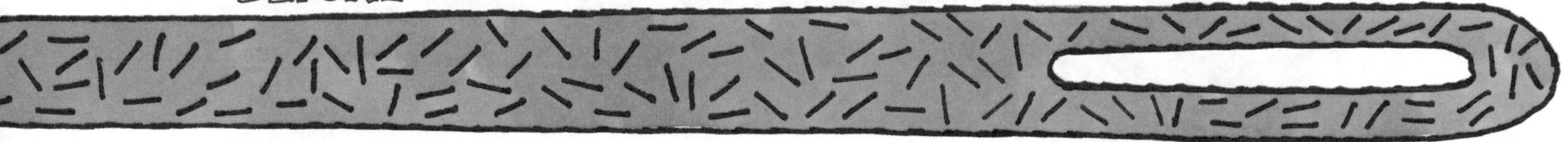

AFTER

But the magnetite from Magnesia is magnetic, and no one stroked it with another magnet. So there must be some other way that things become magnetic.

Magnetite is a natural magnet.

Remember, magnetite contains a lot of iron, and the rocks have been in the ground for thousands of years. Scientists think that the Earth's magnetism has been slowly moving the tiny bits of iron in the rocks, lining them up just as the particles in your needle lined up. This happens because the Earth is a great big magnet. So over thousands of years the Earth may be able to make magnets out of things that have lots of iron in them.

The Earth behaves as though there is a giant magnet inside it.

Magnetism is everywhere on this Earth of ours. It goes through air and water, glass and walls, cardboard and tabletops. You know this because your compass works just about everywhere. Try it and see for yourself.